Mrs. G. R. Alden

Grace Holbrook

And Other Stories of Endeavor and Experience

Mrs. G. R. Alden

Grace Holbrook
And Other Stories of Endeavor and Experience

ISBN/EAN: 9783337141325

Printed in Europe, USA, Canada, Australia, Japan

Cover: Foto ©ninafisch / pixelio.de

More available books at **www.hansebooks.com**

GRACE HOLBROOK

AND OTHER STORIES OF ENDEAVOR AND EXPERIENCE

BY

"PANSY" (Mrs. G. R. Alden)

Author of "Making Fate," "What They Couldn't,"
"Ester Ried," etc., etc.

ILLUSTRATED

BOSTON
LOTHROP PUBLISHING COMPANY

Copyright, 1896,
By LOTHROP PUBLISHING COMPANY.

PANSY
Trade-Mark Registered June 4, 1895.

GRACE HOLBROOK, THE MARTYR.

JENNIE TALBOT was always hunting for four-leaved clovers.

"To be sure, I never find one," she said, with a bright little laugh; "but then, I might, you know, and it's kind of exciting to be always looking."

Rene Holbrook leaned over the fence and watched her, laughing at her for taking so much trouble just for a four-leaved clover. "What good would it do you to find one?" he asked.

"Oh! no good, only they are so uncommon; I think I like things that are a little uncommon. Then it is said to be good luck to find one, you know, though of course I don't believe in luck."

"You believe in wasting your time," said Grace Holbrook, appearing just then from the side piazza. She was sixteen months older than Jennie, and took it upon herself to lecture her occasionally, though the two were seatmates in school, and excellent friends. "I should think you would both better be studying your parts for the Review of Nations, instead of fumbling among those green leaves after silly little clovers. I don't believe either of you are ready for rehearsal."

"I know some of my part," said Jennie, diving in among the younger clovers, and looking curiously at each one in the hope of being rewarded by the sight of a four-leaf; "and I'm going to study all the afternoon. I shall be ready, but I don't like my quotations; they make me shiver. It seems dreadful to have to say over all those terrible things."

"I don't think so," answered Grace, her eyes glowing with excitement. "Your part isn't half so bad as mine, and I like mine. I glory in the courage of those men. Sometimes I almost wish there were martyrs in these days, so we would have a chance to show what we are made of."

Timid little Jennie among the clovers shivered. "Oh! don't," she said, as though wishing might possibly bring it to pass. "I think it was terrible. I am so thankful that I did not live in those days that sometimes I could cry for joy. I almost know I would have been a coward."

"O, Jennie Talbot! you are a pretty girl to have been chosen for that splendid verse you recite about the man who felt the flames creeping up around him. You recite it real well; I don't see how you can, if you feel so."

"It is just because I 'feel so' that I can put feeling into it, I suppose. I can almost seem to see those flames gathering strength, and it makes me feel hot and cold both at once. I am glad, as glad as I can be, that the man could be so splendid; but all the same, I know just as well as I do that I am sitting here in the grass, that I could never have been like him in the world."

"Nonsense!" said Grace loftily; "I could; I feel it in me. I can imagine the whole scene — the trial, and the questions, and the way I should hold up my head and answer, and everything."

A low, chuckling laugh from Rene broke in upon her eloquence. "Much you two know about it," he said. "Just as though you could settle it in these days how you should feel if you were back in the times when it was dangerous to own that you had a Bible, or knew anything about the Bible, or cared anything about it."

Grace turned on him angrily. "Well, I should hope we could, Rene Holbrook. I don't say we can realize it as those people did; but if I couldn't know whether I would be true to my principles and stand up for the Bible, and for everything else that I had promised to uphold, I should be ashamed of myself."

"Well," said Jennie, with a meek little sigh, "I don't feel that way, and I can't. I think I'm a good deal of a coward. I should want to be true, and I think I should try to be; but honestly, I'm afraid I couldn't."

Rene laughed again, this time loud and long; it was so funny to him to hear those girls discussing martyrdom with all the nervous excitement of reality — or of what they imagined was reality — that he could not help but laugh. Grace told him she was ashamed of him, and went away; and soon after gentle little Jennie, who feared that she had in some way offended her dear Grace, followed her example, and went to her own home, which joined the Holbrook house, and set herself about studying her part for the great missionary exercise, which was to be a Review of Nations, and in which exercise she recited a brief descriptive poem concerning the days of the Christian martyrs, with such depth of feeling as to bring tears to the eyes of those who were drilling her. Grace also recited with remarkable power some of the brave, strong answers of those grand men and women, and gloried in the portion of history which she was to represent.

That very evening, at the rehearsal, something occurred which brought the talk in the clover patch vividly back to the three who had lingered there. Some of the little children were being drilled to sing a verse of the old hymn, "There is a Happy Land, Far, Far Away." It was to be sung, during the progress of the Review of Nations, in the Japanese language, as it was sung in their Sabbath-school. Of course much drilling was required to familiarize the little singers with those queer-sounding syllables which made them feel like laughing.

Meantime the older ones, who were waiting for their turn to rehearse, scattered in groups, and amused themselves as best they could. In one group of half a dozen boys, and more than that number of girls, were Grace Holbrook and her brother, and Jennie Talbot. Over and over were the sweet, familiar strains of the old hymn which every one of these had sung in childhood repeated.

"I should think those chicks had had time to learn a million verses of the thing," said one of the boys at last, impatiently. "If they would try our words it wouldn't take so long, would it, Rene?"

"What are your words?" asked Grace. And in reply Rene sang in undertone, to the tune of "Happy Land":

> "There is a boarding-house,
>   Not far away,
> Where they have ham and eggs
>   Three times a day."

Several of the girls, who had not heard this remarkable parody before, were convulsed with laughter. Grace Holbrook laughed with the rest, though there was a little flush on her cheek. The boys to whom the trash was familiar looked on in smiling enjoyment, and only little Jennie Talbot, her cheeks red, and her heart beating fast because of the courage it took, said timidly, though quite distinctly: "Boys, I don't believe it is right to sing such silly words to that hymn tune."

Rene opened his great brown eyes wider than usual.

"Why not?" he asked. "Tunes aren't sacred. What earthly harm can it do?"

"Well, for one thing it will make people think of those words the next time they hear the tune, and then they will feel like laughing. Then there are other reasons which I can feel, but cannot tell. I don't believe it is quite right; you never hear real good people do it. Don't you believe you would be shocked if Dr. Grierson should sing it that way, just for fun?"

"Oh! I wouldn't have him do it in prayer meeting," answered Rene loftily.

"No; I don't mean in prayer meeting; I mean here at rehearsal. If he should come along now singing 'Happy Land,' and when he came near enough we should find it was to those words, would you think it was real nice?"

"Dr. Grierson is a minister," said Rene shortly, "and I am not." Then he turned away, looking cross. There was quite a little discussion about the matter, but Jennie said no more. As for Grace, her eyes had flashed a good deal, but she did not say much until they were walking home together, she and Rene and Jennie Talbot. Then she began.

"I don't think it was very nice in you, Jennie Talbot, to lecture those boys who are so much older than you. Rene didn't mind it, of course; but there was John Moore, nearly three years older than you; he was singing, too, and he looked ever so annoyed."

"I didn't mean to lecture," said Jennie gently; "I didn't want to say a word; and at first I thought I would laugh it off with the rest; but I truly think it is wrong, and it did not seem right to keep still."

"Nonsense!" said Grace severely; "as if it would have done any harm to laugh. I didn't admire the stuff myself; but I don't think it is necessary to set myself up above other people and lecture them. My way is to just laugh such things off and forget them, and I don't believe " —

"Oh! hold on now, Sis." It was Rene's voice that interrupted. "I'm the fellow who deserved the most of the scolding, so I have a right to speak; it was the gentlest little scolding ever heard of, and made me feel ashamed of myself. If it is any pleasure to Jennie to know it, I quite agree with her; 'Happy Land' has too many tender memories to be associated with such trash as we were getting off to-night. Moreover, I may as well tell you what I specially thought of; that Jennie had gone back to our morning's talk, and was living out some of the ideas advanced. I've made up my mind which of us three would have the courage to be a martyr if the chance offered, and it wouldn't be a person by the name of Holbrook, in my opinion. Anybody could see it took a lot of courage for you to speak up in the way you did, Jennie. And as for John Moore, since we are on the subject and talking plainly, I'll tell you what he said:

"'That's a first-class little heroine, isn't it? I tell you what it is, she is going to stand up for what she thinks is right every time, if it does make her cheeks red.'"

And then, to Grace Holbrook's relief, they reached her father's door, and she was not obliged to make any reply to these astonishing revelations.

CELIA STUART'S TRUST.

SHE was a pretty girl when her face was pleasant, but this morning it was all in a frown. In vain Baby Frances made her prettiest attempts at speech, Celia would not smile. Something was the matter with one of the wheels to Baby Frances' carriage, so the willow top had been taken off and set on the floor, with Frances in it, and Celia had been called to amuse her, while the wheels went to the carriage maker's to be repaired. As a general thing Celia was ready to play with Baby Frances, but this morning she was not. Carrie Wheelock, her next-door neighbor, had company, two little girls with curls and dollies; they were out in the yard at this moment having a party for their dollies, and Celia had intended to take her Amelia Jane and go and call upon them. In her secret heart she believed that Amelia Jane was better looking and better dressed than any of the other dollies, but she could not be quite sure until she had a nearer view. It was very trying, just as she had Amelia Jane dressed in her best, and was going out of the door, to be called back to Frances. Celia could never remember feeling so thoroughly out of humor as she did when she slammed her dollie on the floor, and told her sharply to "lie still and behave herself!" and then sat down in a sullen little heap in front of Frances. She was half-frightened at the thoughts which floated through her mind. "I'm sick and tired of taking care of Frances! I just wish she had some wings and would fly away." I suppose what made her think of this, was the fact that two bright-winged birds at that moment flew past the window and alighted on one of the limbs of the great oak-tree. Celia reflected that Frances would look very pretty in her white dress, seated up there among the green leaves. Frances, however, not being a bird, wanted to be amused, and puckered her lip when she found Celia was not going to amuse her.

"Hush up!" said that young woman, speaking sharply; "it is bad enough to have to stay in the house and take care of you, without having you cry about it."

Just then she heard a shout of laughter from the yard next door. Celia's curiosity got the better of her. "I'll just run to the door and see what they are laughing about," she said, springing up; "nothing can happen to Frances in such a little minute as that."

"O, Celia!" called Carrie, the minute the side door opened and Celia's head appeared, "do come here and see what we found in the china bowl in our playhouse."

"I can't," said Celia; "I have Baby to take care of. What did you find?" and she moved three steps toward the next yard. She did not mean to do it, but they held up something for her to see, and she could not see it; she took three steps more, and at last was fairly inside the yard, gazing at the curious flying bug with great green wings, that had set up housekeeping in the china bowl. After that it could do no harm merely to glance at the dollies and see if they were in any way superior to Amelia Jane. In her own opinion she staid a very short time indeed, then ran back as fast as she could, expecting to hear Frances scream as she neared the sitting-room. But no sound reached her ears. She pushed open the door in breathless haste. There lay Amelia Jane on the floor where she had thrown her, but in the willow carriage top sat Frisk and Whisk, looking as full of mischief as their names suggested. But where was Frances? I do not think poor Celia ever forgot the feeling which came over her as she saw the kittens in Baby's place, and realized that Baby was gone. For a moment it seemed to her as though her heart stopped beating. The next, she gave a scream which could have been heard away out at the stables.

"O, mamma! what has become of Frances?"

Through the house she ran, screaming louder with every step, until Ann caught hold of her arm and spoke with authority. "For pity's sake, Miss Celia, stop your yelling. You will scare your mamma to pieces, and set the baby into fits. Whatever is the matter?"

"The baby!" screamed Celia. "Somebody has carried her off."

"Why, what ails the child? The baby is in her mamma's arms this minute going to sleep, or trying to, if you don't scare her out of it."

"O, Ann! are you sure mamma has her?"

"Sure? of course I am. Didn't I just take her up a glass of water? Sit down, child, and get your breath; you are all of a tremble. What did you think had happened?"

"I didn't know," said Celia, and she dropped in a little heap on the floor and began to cry.

"Mamma," said the little girl that evening, after several things had been explained, "do you think perhaps God had you take Frances out of her carriage just then, and let Frisk and Whisk come in her place to scare me and punish me? He wouldn't do that, would he, when he could see right into my heart, and knew I did not mean it at all; that I would not have her fly away for anything in the world?"

Mamma bent over her work-basket for a moment to hide a smile. Celia's idea some way sounded very odd. Presently she answered:

"I think, dear, that God may have let Frisk and Whisk help to teach you a lesson. You were given a trust; you know, and were not faithful to it. Serious things might have happened to Frances even in that short time, which was not so short as it seemed to you. If the fright you had has taught you to be faithful when you are called to take a responsibility, you will have reason to thank the kittens for their share in the day's lesson, will you not?"

Celia smiled somewhat gravely; but the next moment she shivered as she said: "O, mamma! wouldn't it have been dreadful if He had given her wings, and she had flown up in a tree, and we could not get her down?"

"Poor little girlie," said her mother, "your nerves need resting. If I were you I would go to bed, and to sleep. God will take care of Frances, and you, and the birdies, and everybody."

POOR MAMIE.

IT came over her all at once while she was dressing — not by any means for the first time, either. Nobody but she knew how many tears she had shed over this trouble which had come upon her; but on this first of April morning, with the sun shining brightly outside, and the birds singing their welcome to spring, it seemed harder than ever. At the risk of rumpling her pretty hair, which she had arranged neatly, Mamie threw herself in a disconsolate heap on her bed, buried her head in the pillow, and cried as though her heart would break.

What great trouble had come to Mamie? I am sure you will not laugh when I tell you; it was no laughing matter.

An "April-fool party" had been in the air for the past three weeks. Mamie's particular friend, Estelle Burton, was to give it, and fifty girls and boys were invited. Great preparations had been made, for Estelle's father was a rich man, and could afford to spend a good deal of money to please his daughter.

"She is well worth pleasing," he used to say, with a nod of his head, when he saw her pretty figure skipping across the lawn. "She is well worth pleasing, if she was born on April-fool's Day."

Estelle was a year older than Mamie — thirteen this April day.

Perhaps you do not know what an "April-fool's party" is?

I suspect it is anything that the persons planning choose to make it. Estelle's was to be very interesting and delightful. Mamie was in all the secrets, had been one of the helpers, indeed, and knew just how charming it was to be. To begin with, the elegant supper which had been prepared was not to be served in the dining-room. When the call to supper came, and the guests filed out, they were to find nothing in the dining-room but the ordinary furniture; the great dining-table, made as small as possible, and strewn with books and papers, instead of with good things to eat. The guests were to be informed that they would have to hunt for their supper. Then the way they would scamper over that great, handsome house, after they had been given leave to search in every room whose door was closed, Mamie could readily imagine. They were to be earnestly cautioned on no account to set foot in a room whose door stood open—everything about that wonderful April-fool party had been planned to go by contraries. At last, on the third floor back, in a room which had been used once as a nursery, the guests would find the table set with elegance, and covered with all sorts of delightful surprises.

The English walnuts were to be carefully split open, their meats removed, and in their places choice bits of French candies fitted; then the edges were to be touched with mucilage, and made to look as though the nuts were not yet cracked. In the center of the table was to be a huge dish piled high with potatoes very much baked. Such a queer dish for a birthday party! But every guest was to be urged by all means to take one, and very glad would they be to have done so; for they would find that the potato had been carefully scraped out, and in its place there would be found a pretty gift for each to carry home. Oh! it was to be as charming an April-fool party as had ever been planned.

Mamie had enjoyed it all so much. It had been so pleasant to be taken into the secrets, and to be consulted as to this or that plan. It had given her a position of importance among the girls; they had asked her as many questions as they had Estelle, and seemed to understand that she was quite as well posted. What was there in all this to land poor Mamie on her bed and make her bury her head in the pillow?

The trouble was all about a dress. Every girl in her class was to appear at the party in a new spring dress, and Mamie's heart had been set upon having one for the occasion. Her mother had done what she could to make her daughter think that the neat blue dress she had worn for best all winter would be the most suitable for a party so early in the season. She had reminded her that it was too late to buy a winter dress, and too early for a summer one. At last they had compromised. Aunt

Kate's pretty cashmere skirt, the front breadth of which had been ruined by coffee, had been presented to Mamie, and her mother had bought silk enough to make it up with. This was almost as good as a new dress, though not quite, for poor Mamie, who had not a great deal of moral courage in some directions, could seem to see Mabel Blair's great black eyes as she examined the dress from head to foot, and hear her high-keyed voice as she asked, "Is your dress every speck new, or is it made over from one of your mother's?" For Mabel Blair had not been well brought up, and did not know that such questions were rude.

The bitter tears were being caused by the fact that a message had come from the dressmaker's but the evening before, that one of her girls was ill, and another had been called home to wait upon a sick mother, and therefore the dress could not possibly be ready in time. I am obliged to confess that for the next few hours Mamie made every one around her uncomfortable. She had half a dozen impracticable schemes for finishing that dress, which had to be discussed and abandoned one by one.

Her mother was very patient and sympathetic. If her "thimble finger" had not been sore she would have sent for the dress and finished it herself, despite all her other duties; if Aunt Kate hadn't gone to Boston by the early train she would have finished it for her. If they could afford to send it to Madame Rainsford and pay her very high price possibly it might be done; but that was out of the question.

"You know, Mamie dear," said the mother, "I strained a point to get the silk, and father has had heavy expenses this spring; we must not even think of Madame Rainsford. Try not to care about it, little daughter; your blue dress is very neat and appropriate."

But Mamie's face was all in a frown. "I don't care a bit about the old dress now," she said; "it doesn't make any difference if it is never finished. If I can't have it for the party I don't want it ever."

As a rule Mamie spoke the truth, but these words she knew were not true. Sore as her heart was, if she had thought that the pretty dress would never be finished, it would have been sorer still. As it was, she cried half a dozen times before the morning was over, and began the new month in a shower of tears. It was not that she did not consider her blue dress quite respectable, although she had given it a kick the night before and called it "that old thing;" it was simply the feeling that all the other girls had new dresses to wear, and that possibly Mabel Blair would say to her before all the girls, "I thought you was going to have a new dress for to-day. Didn't you hate to come in the dress you have worn to church all winter?" Mamie believed this would be "too dreadful."

It took so much time to cry, and then to try to remove the traces of tears, that the breakfast-bell rang before she was ready, and she had to go down without her daily Bible reading and prayer. A bad beginning, certainly; no wonder that Satan had the best of it all that morning.

Her mother was very patient; she was sorry for the little red-eyed, foolish girl, and tried to make life as endurable for her as she could.

But Mamie on her part made no such effort. She said she did not want an egg for breakfast, she was tired of the sight of eggs; and the toast was scorched; she did not see why they always had to have scorched toast. Nobody reminded her of the untruthfulness of this hint, because everybody saw that it was not Mamie who was speaking, but an evil spirit who for the time being had possession of her.

It is surprising how many disagreeable things one can find in life if one sets out to look for them. Nothing was right in or about Mamie's home. It was "the most tucked-up house" she ever saw. She was sure she could not clear up the sitting-room; there were no places to put things. John had his boxes on the shelves where they did not belong, and Sarah was so cross when she went to the kitchen for something that she did not want to go again.

"Don't you want me to put some of this lace in your dress, dear?" her mother asked, as she took from her drawer a bit of choice old lace that belonged to herself.

"No, ma'am," said Mamie drearily; "I don't think I shall go to the party. I can't wear that old dress when all the others will be in new ones."

"O, daughter!" said her mother; "I am sorry you cannot rise above such unworthy feelings, and be happy in spite of your disappointment."

"O, now, mamma! you don't know anything about it; if you were a little girl you would understand. I have real trying times all the while. The girls I go with dress a great deal nicer than I; they have new, stylish things, and I have to go looking like an old dowdy. I'm tired of it; I wish we had money enough to do like other people, or else didn't have to go with them. I wish we lived away out in the woods, and never got invited to parties, or anywhere."

"O, no, daughter! I don't think you really wish that. Come to the window and see this sweet-faced girl in the carriage across the street. I have been looking at her for several minutes. She is just about your age, and her face is as sweet and quiet as a flower."

Mamie came to the window with the frown still on her face.

"O, yes!" she said; "I know who that girl is. No wonder she is sweet — what has she got to make her anything else? They are the Easterwoods, from Boston; they board at the hotel, and are just as rich as they can be. They brought their own servants, and horses, and carriage, and everything. See what a lovely carriage it is, and look how elegantly the little girl is dressed. How would I look sitting beside her in that old blue dress that you think is so nice? All she has to do is to be prinked up like a doll, and ride around in that splendid carriage with a coachman to wait on her, and a servant to do just as she says. They say she has a servant with her all the time."

"So that is your idea of happiness, is it, dear?" Mrs. Hood looked half-amused, half-reproachful; she hardly knew her daughter in this mood, for though inclined to be a trifle envious sometimes, Mamie seldom allowed her evil thoughts to get the better of her as they had this morning.

"I don't care!" she said, in answer to the reproach in her mother's tone, "it would make a difference; you know it would. Don't you believe if I had such pretty things as that girl has, and could ride around in a carriage, I should be happy? I know I should; I just love beautiful things, and I hardly ever have any. Mother, the carriage is stopping here!"

This last sentence was spoken in a tone of excitement, with all the fretful gone out of it.

"They are probably in search of some one they cannot find," said Mrs. Hood. She went at once to the door, Mamie following, and standing on the little porch, where she could hear the conversation. Mrs. Easterwood wanted to ask about a girl who had once worked for Mrs. Hood, and the two ladies stood talking for some minutes.

Mamie could not help observing that Mrs. Easterwood was very courteous to her mother, treating her as well as though she had been dressed in silk, instead of a plain morning gingham. The fact is, Mamie had yet to learn that really refined people do not gauge their treatment of others by the style of dress they wear.

"Do you think the young woman would be able to do plain sewing, like the repairing of garments?" the lady asked; "my daughter needs some work of that kind." And she turned tender eyes upon the fair-faced girl at her side.

"As to that," said Mrs. Hood, "I am not prepared to answer. Perhaps you would like to come in and see her? She is at my house now; her sister is helping me for a few days, and she has come to spend the morning with her; you could perhaps judge better about her by seeing her at her work. Meantime, would your daughter like to take a walk around our yard and look at some of the early spring flowers?"

"O, dear me!" said Mamie, from the piazza, "what can mamma mean by asking that elegant girl to walk around our little country yard? I hope I sha'n't have to go and speak to her; I should be frightened out of my senses. I wish mamma wouldn't."

But Mrs. Easterwood was speaking again, the tender look in her eyes deepening as they rested sadly on her daughter. "She would like it above all things, dear madam; but it is quite out of her power. My daughter cannot take a step. It is four years since she has even stood, without being carefully supported on either side."

There followed earnest words of sympathy, and a few tender questions were asked and answered.

"Yes," said Mrs. Easterwood, laying her hand lovingly on her daughter's arm, "Mamie has been very patient through all these months and years of suffering. I have never heard a murmur from her lips; it is truly wonderful how she has been sustained."

A few minutes afterwards the carriage rolled away, and Mrs. Hood came slowly up the walk, her eyes on the ground, and they were dim with tears.

Her daughter flew down the steps to meet her, and Mrs. Hood put her arms about her and smoothed the hair from her face, as she said tenderly, "Poor Mamie!"

"Which one, mamma dear?" asked Mamie softly.

"Which one does my daughter think?"

"O, mamma, dear mamma! the other one. I am so sorry for her. How can she be patient? I never could. But O, mamma! I am so ashamed. I will never fret any more about my dress, or anything; I will be just as grateful and glad as I can be. Only think of not being able to take a step.

"Poor Mamie!"

HOW KATIE "ENDEAVORED."

"COME on, Katie!" called the girls who were waiting at the gate. "What does make you so slow? It's awfully hot standing here in the sun."

Then Katie appeared at the door. "Go on, girls, please, I can't come just yet; I'll follow you."

"Why, you'll miss the boat! we have just time to get there."

"Well, then, I shall," said Katie resolutely; 'I'm not coming, now; I've something to do."

It was a very warm day. Father had just come in from the field; he looked utterly tired out as he sank into a chair and fanned himself with his hat. "Whew!" he said, "this day is a scorcher."

"You feel it more," said Katie's mother anxiously, "because you ate almost nothing for dinner; I wish they knew how to fix something nourishing for you." Then she sighed. She was lying on the couch, and knew that she must lie there and not go into the kitchen on any account. All this Katie heard, while she was getting a clean handkerchief and making ready for a ten-cent trip on the little lake steamer with the girls, to "cool off." Then she thought of something. It was that which made her dart out to the girls and tell them to go on without her. This they did, grumbling. Katie went into the kitchen. From Norah she got an egg, helped herself to a bowl, put in it a teaspoonful of sugar and one of lemon juice; then she dropped in the yolk of the egg and beat it to a foam. The white of the egg she had put on a plate; she added to it a pinch of salt, then with the fine wire egg-beater made a wonderful foam of it, and poured it over the yolk. Now for a tumbler. The lovely foamy liquid was lightly poured into it, and Katie ran to her father with the glass.

"Here is something very good and nourishing for you to drink," she said eagerly. And while father tasted, and tasted, and sipped, and smacked his lips, the mother looking on well pleased, said: "Where did you learn to make it, dear? Why, I thought you were going up the lake with the girls."

"It was in our cooking lesson this very morning, mamma. I thought I wouldn't go to the shore this time."

"I promised to do just what Jesus would like to have me," said Katie to herself that evening as the girls stopped to tell her what a good time they had, "and I think he liked me to help rest papa."

A CHRISTIAN ENDEAVOR PICNIC.

THE little boats near at hand and the larger boats in the distance danced and fluttered like things of life on the clear sparkling water, and tried in vain to arrest Dorothea's attention. She had settled herself in on her camp stool in her favorite position for watching the boats and the sky, and she had a half-opened book in hand as though she might be planning to read when weary of watching; but neither book nor boat held her thoughts this morning. Something of more importance than either had her in charge, and perplexed her not a little. There was quite a large party of them gathered at the one large boarding-house in the quiet country town whose only apparent attraction was the sea. People wondered how Dorothea Conklin could interest herself in such a dull, sleepy old place. But Dorothea had been here with her auntie for two years, and liked to come; and this season she had brought down with her a bevy of cousins, and friends of cousins, who were making the old farm boarding-house merry from morning to night.

They were doing more than that. Eurie Shipley was among the number, and Eurie never went anywhere without remembering that she was a member of the Christian Endeavor Society, and pledged to service. It was Eurie, with the intelligent and persistent help of her cousin Earle, who had planned the scheme which was giving Dorothea perplexed thoughts. This was no more nor less than to district the sleepy little town in which they found themselves for a six weeks' stay, apportioning a certain quarter of the town to each Endeavorer, whose business it would be to make the acquaintance of all the young people they saw or heard of lying within their district, and invite them cordially to the Christian Endeavor meeting which was to be held in the dining-room of the boarding-house each Friday evening. Some of the Endeavorers had exclaimed over the plan as being not suited to the place they were in.

"It is not likely they ever heard of such a

creature as a Christian Endeavorer," Katie Stuart had said; "they won't know what to make of us." It was Dorothea who had answered quickly, "So much the more need, then, for your telling them what such a creature is, and what she wants to accomplish."

Dorothea had approved of the plan from the first; it was only this morning that she had awakened to the fact that there were embarrassments connected with it. A little farther up the beach she had stopped to watch the strong arms of Farmer Hemple's daughter Katrine skillfully push her boat through the breakers to the shore, and admired the strength and skill with which she managed it. Katrine's boat was laden with all sorts of treasures, which she was evidently going to try to sell to the strangers in town, and so earn a little money, perhaps, for herself. She was dressed in the rough costume of a fisherman's daughter, and it would have taken much wetting to have penetrated through her thick boots. Dorothea had watched her before bring her boat safely through those terrible breakers, and had thought only of the strength she was developing, and about what an honest, intelligent face she had. This morning she thought, with a little start of dismay, that Katrine Hempel belonged to her division. She knew just where the little old weather-beaten cottage stood in which fisherman Hempel lived, and it was without doubt in the district set apart to her. How was she to invite a girl like Katrine to a Christian Endeavor prayer meeting? The thing seemed so incongruous, so almost ridiculous. She had never spoken to the girl in her life, and to walk up to her and ask her to come to the boarding-house to a prayer meeting seemed almost impossible. Yet was not this what she was pledged to do?

She had turned away from the beach and gone toward the boarding-house, thinking her perplexed thoughts, and had not found relief by coming suddenly upon a group of three, who had gathered under the trees for a visit. Queer-looking creatures they were, judged by Miss Dorothea's ideas of things. Two of them had German faces, and were coarsely, even oddly dressed. But one, with a little more refinement of face and manner, had a large magazine in her lap, and seemed to have been reading something aloud; for as Dorothea approached she heard the boy say in discontented tones: "I don't know what it means, I am sure; something going on in the world, I suppose, that we know nothing about. We never get a chance to learn things, any of us."

"There are a good many strangers at the farm," the reader had replied, and her voice sounded wistful. "Perhaps we will have a chance to find out some things from them."

But the boy shook his head. "They are no good," he said; "they are stuck-ups, and don't care anything about folks like us."

And Dorothea, just as he turned his head in her direction, saw that he was Henry Myers, the boy who often rowed around the point with the mail; one girl must be his sister, and the other was doubtless the cousin of whom she had heard her landlady speak the other day. And then Dorothea felt the blood rolling in waves into her face as she remembered that the Myers were also in her district. She had entirely forgotten their little house down by the woods, and had told herself that she would have an easy time in her division, because there were so few houses, and almost no young people. Here were several young people whom she did not in the least know how to manage. It was of no use to try to put them out of her mind, for she had taken the pledge with the rest to do her part, and had heartily sustained the proposition from the first. Some plan between this and Friday must be devised for making it seem natural and sensible in her to invite these young people whom she had met and passed dozens of times and never spoken to, to attend their prayer meeting.

She went at last to her sheltered spot where we found her, but neither watched the boats nor read her paper; instead, she thought and thought.

I don't know where the startling suggestion came from, but it came.

The boarding-house party, who had occupied themselves that morning with separate interests, were to go in the afternoon to a certain wood about a mile from the farmhouse in search of ferns and mosses, and other wood treasures with which to decorate the dining-room, ready for Friday evening. At least that was the reason they talked about; perhaps the real reason was that they wanted a frolic; and they had coaxed Mrs. Simms, the landlady, into planning a choice supper for them, which was to be eaten in the woods.

This was Dorothea's thought: "Why not invite Katrine, and Henry, and the others to go with us? They are about our age, and are almost the only young people around here who are not busy with farm work just now. They know the woods, of course, and could probably show us the best places for finding nice things, and perhaps they would enjoy spending an afternoon with us and having supper together. After that I think I should have the face to invite them to prayer meeting."

The thought grew as she studied it, and finally took such possession of her that she went in search of Eurie Shipley and the others to propose it.

She nearly took their breaths away. Even Eurie Shipley seemed dismayed for a moment, and Katie Stuart said: "What an idea! you do go to such lengths, Dorothea."

There was a great deal of talking, and some opposition, of course; but it ended by Dorothea doing just that thing. Four more astonished young people than were those who received their invitation at noon of that same day, could hardly be imagined.

"The woods?" said Katrine, her strong brown face growing a deep red as she spoke. "Of course I know all about them; I'll go and show you where to find the maiden-hair ferns, but I couldn't stay to supper; that would be ridiculous."

"O, yes, indeed!" said Dorothea, and her voice was eager. She was growing not only willing to invite these strangers, but very anxious to have them accept. "We must have you stay; we want you very much; we are just going to have a nice pleasant frolic, and we know we shall enjoy it more if you will come; it is just girls and boys, you know; there is nobody to be afraid of."

Katrine laughed. She felt more afraid of girls and boys who belonged to that charmed world in which she did not live than of any men and women she had ever seen. But Dorothea had a very coaxing way with her when she chose, and it ended in Katrine's not only promising to go, but to " make " the others do the same. The girl was a power in her circle; but she had a harder time than Dorothea ever knew anything about. At first Henry Myers declared that he "couldn't," and "wouldn't," and "nobody need ask him." However, he did.

You want to know if the picnic was a success? My dears, I want to know if you ever heard of girls like Dorothea and Eurie Shipley and two or three of the others putting their minds and hearts to a project and not making a success of it?

"Of course it is the way to do," Eurie Shipley said, after her first gasp of astonishment was over, and she had had time to think. "We cannot expect these young people to be burning with a desire to accept invitations to our prayer meetings, when we ignore them all the rest of the time. We ought to make the picnics, and all the other things, help along the main object. I vote to have Dorothea invite them heartily, in the name of us all; and I'm willing to give

THE CHRISTIAN ENDEAVOR PICNIC.

her a vote of thanks for being sweet enough to think of it."

"I didn't think of it," said Dorothea, with earnest gravity. "I — well, to tell you the truth, I was praying a little sentence, to ask to be shown how to invite them to the prayer meeting, and it just came to me as an answer, you know."

Katie Stuart had her lips open to offer another objection, but after that closed them. If this really was an answer to Dorothea's prayer, why then —

And to these young people who believed in answers to prayer there really seemed nothing more to be said.

Katrine Hempel wore a white dress which was rather short and rather coarse, but it was clean and neat; and her honest, sensible face was wreathed with smiles when she found she could tell the young people a great many interesting things about mosses and ferns and lichens; and Henry Myers went off for a quiet stroll with Robert Weston, and mustered courage to ask a few questions about something he had read in the paper, and received a flood of light in return, and the promise of a book which would tell him the whole story; and he promised to give Robert a lesson in surf-rowing the next day.

I may as well own that Henry Myers, who had heard of the plan of districting the neighborhood, had said on Monday that he wouldn't go to their prayer meeting if they went down on their knees and begged him to; that they were "all a set of stuck-ups" with whom he wanted nothing to do. And he said on Friday morning, when he received his invitation, that he would certainly come if he could.

And he could, and did. When the merry party from the city completed their six weeks' vacation and went home, they left a Christian Endeavor Society in the quiet seaside village fully organized, and Henry Myers and Katrine Hempel are both on the lookout committee.

WHEN I WAS A GIRL.

I REMEMBER the day distinctly. I can seem to feel again how my head ached, and how the veins about my temples throbbed as I hurried home from school, rushed into the house, made a dash for my mother's room, threw myself on the floor beside her chair, and burying my face in my hands, let the sobs which had seemed to be almost choking me have full vent. I can seem to feel the touch of my mother's hand upon my head, and hear her gentle voice:

"Dear little girl! What has happened to her? Tell mother all about it."

My mother's voice was the sweetest music the world had for me. I have a picture of her looking very much as she did that day, sitting in the large old-fashioned high-backed chair, her hair combed smoothly away from her forehead, and caught back with tortoise-shell side combs. She wore a high back comb, also of tortoise shell, which securely held the coil of hair wound about it. Mother never was very well or strong, and we girls generally found her in her high-backed chair when we came home. Every one of us was in the habit of seeking her, to give the history of our joys and sorrows. Poor mother! how many stories she must have had to hear, and how constantly her sympathies were drawn upon. We did not think of it in those days; we took it as a matter of course. But this particular day stands out vividly in my memory. I had had a harder time than usual. I can tell the story straighter now than I did to my mother, for then it was constantly interrupted by sobs and fresh bursts of tears. There was a girl at school who had pretty yellow curls and a pretty doll face. She was a favorite with some of the scholars, but not with me. From the very first day I met her, there seemed to be a conflict between us. Yet we were in the same classes, and often thrown together. The truth is, I suspect we were in some ways rivals, which made us both uncomfortable. Of all the girls in our class, Phebe and I were the only ones who liked to write compositions; the others groaned and sighed over them, wished that the weeks were a month long, so that every other Friday would not come so often. But to Phebe and me those Friday afternoons were looked forward with interest. Up to the time of my coming into the school Phebe had been altogether the best writer — perhaps that is not saying a great deal, for the others disliked the work so much that they made no effort to excel. Phebe had a vivid imagination, and knew a number of facts which she delighted to weave into story form, and read as compositions. Both girls and boys liked to listen to them much better than they did to papers about "spring" and "flowers," such as the others wrote.

Now it happened that I had been trained almost from my babyhood to do this very thing. "Make a story out of it for mother," was a most familiar sentence. Before I could write, I was encouraged to tell a story for mother out of a picture which I brought to show her, or perhaps out of two or three blocks, or a few flowers. The consequence was that when I was a girl of thirteen and began to go to school, it was more natural for me to express my thoughts on paper in story form than in any other way. And naturally I became a powerful rival to Phebe, who had had no training, and only followed her own fancies. I remember the first story I read before the assembled scholars of a bright Friday afternoon; and I remember that Phebe was the only girl there who did not seem to like it. The others flocked about me and said it was "perfectly lovely," and "just splendid," and all those words which schoolgirls like to use; but Phebe tossed her yellow curls, and declared she did not think it amounted to much.

It was on a Friday that my heart was broken. I had been selected again to read; not only before the entire school, but in the presence of the trustees as well, and of several other visitors. There was always a selection made from the pupils for this honor. Only six boys and six girls, out of the several hundred which composed our school, could be heard in the chapel on Friday afternoons. I suspect it had been the custom for some time to select Phebe whenever there was any prospect of company; but on this particular afternoon I was chosen, and Phebe was not. I read my story, which was really a very silly little thing; for don't you believe I came across a copy of it but a few weeks ago, and laughed and cried over the memories connected with it, and said between the tears and the laughter, "The idea that I ever could have supposed that there was anything in this worth crying over." But it seemed a very excellent thing to me then; and many of the girls and boys thought so, too. Well, I read it — thanks to my mother's training, I was a fairly good reader. I had more compliments than usual, and I suppose was somewhat puffed up. I remember wondering, as I went to answer a summons to Professor Barnard's room, whether he might not be going to say to me that he considered me an honor to the school, or something of that sort. Professor Barnard was our principal. We younger girls saw very little of him, and had immense respect for him. He looked very grave as I came in; not at all as if he were going to say anything complimentary. It took him some time to explain why I had been sent for. I was so bewildered by his first words that it made me stupid. At last, however, I understood. That girl Phebe had actually been to Professor Barnard with a statement that my composition was not original; was, in fact, stolen! She had declared to him that she had a book at home in which was every word in my composition.

This statement was repeated so earnestly, Phebe even declaring that she was willing to bring the book to school and show it to me, that Professor Barnard was troubled. He had known Phebe a long time, and had had no reason to doubt her word; and she was a bright smart girl, and generally knew what she was talking about; it was only too evident that he thought she must be right. How shall I describe to you the storm of passion into which his words put me? I realize now how very suspicious this must have seemed to Professor Barnard. How he probably said to himself, "If this little girl is innocent, why does she not quietly and earnestly explain to me that there is some mistake, and that she certainly wrote her composition herself, without help from any book, instead of getting into such a rage, and talking so fast that I can hardly understand what she says, even stamping her foot?" Yes; I remember I stamped my foot, not at Professor Barnard, but at the very thought of Phebe. I spent my breath in trying to explain what I thought of such a dreadful, dreadful girl. At last Professor Barnard interrupted with: "That will do, Isabella. Do not speak another word. You are not in condition to talk properly."

How well I remember his language. "This is a very grave charge, and we must investigate it fully. I think you know me well enough to be sure that you will not be condemned without positive proof. Unfortunately Phebe lives too far away to be sent home for the book, and as it is Friday afternoon we shall have to let the matter rest until Monday. But I will direct her to bring the book to me on Monday morning and show me the story which she thinks the same as yours. If they are very much alike you shall explain to me, if you can, how you think it may have happened. It is possible, that you may have read a story and forgotten about it. Such things have occurred."

But at this I was so indignant that I was very near stamping my foot again. "I never did!" I said excitedly; "I never, never read a story like mine."

"Hush!" said Professor Barnard, "you are not to say another word about this matter in the school building. Do not speak to the scholars on the subject; if I hear of your doing so I shall be greatly displeased. And now, as it is nearly time for closing, and you are through with your work for the day, I will excuse you at once. I advise you to go directly home. I am very sorry that you have allowed yourself to get into such a passion. The matter is serious enough, without adding to it in this way."

His words hurt me. Perhaps it is no wonder that I remember them well. I had never been reproved by Professor Barnard before. So this is the story that I sobbed out to my mother; and all the while her gentle caressing hand was on my head.

"Poor little girl!" she said, "mother is very sorry that you were angry." I staid my tears to look up at her with astonishment.

"Why, mother," I said, "how could I help being angry? You would have been angry yourself. What do you mean, mother? Don't you know that it is not true?"

"Certainly, my daughter, mother knows, and so does her little girl. Such being the case, why should you become angry at a simple mistake?"

"Mistake!" I repeated indignantly, "there is no mistake about it. It is just her mean ugly way; she is jealous of me, and took this way to make me have a horrid time. I know just what she will do, she will say that the book is lost; that she cannot find it anywhere, or that somebody who was visiting them from a thousand miles away has carried it off. Oh! I know her; she will slip out of it in some way, and make everybody think that I stole my story. The professor thinks so now; I know he does." Then I remember that I buried my face again in my mother's lap, and cried harder than ever. Oh! what a time it was. And what a dreadful Sunday we had. I think I made everybody in the house miserable. Poor mother was sick, and could not go to church, and I staid with her; but I gave her very little peace. I remember I had moments of trying to be submissive to my fate. I even made up a story about a girl who rose above a like trial, and showed such a beautiful spirit that in the end she obliged everybody to see that she had been a martyr. But it was easier to make a story about it than it was to live it. The greater portion of the time I was going over every little detail of the trouble, trying to plan what I should say the next morning. I remember that the day seemed a very long one. I looked anxiously forward to Monday morning, and at the same time dreaded it. I went to school armed with a letter from my mother, carefully written, in her pretty delicate hand, on the very prettiest note-paper she had. It explained to Professor Barnard that I wrote my composition sitting by her side, and that I proposed and rejected several ways of finishing the story, even writing one or two of them out before I finally settled on the plan which suited me. In proof of this she inclosed the first writing, on scraps of paper, just as I had scribbled them. I might have been saved all my agony and ill-temper if I had remembered what strong proofs these were of my truthfulness. Directly after prayers I was summoned to Professor Barnard's private room — the place where scholars always went to receive either special praise or special scoldings.

Phebe was there, her curls looking more golden than ever in the bright sunlight; and I thought her eyes danced wickedly. Professor Barnard motioned us both to seats in front of of him, and said: "Well, Phebe, you remember, I suppose, what I told you you must bring me to-day. Are you ready to do so?"

"Yes, sir," said Phebe, very promptly; "I brought it, and Isabella's story is in it word for word, just as I said. It is on the shelf in the hall; the book is so big that I could not bring it into chapel with me. May I go and get it?"

I could hardly believe my ears. The professor bowed his head, and Phebe tripped out, coming back in a moment with a great book, which she carried to the desk, my heart beating so meantime that it seemed as though the professor must hear it. I suppose it was only a moment or two, but as I remember it, it seemed to me at least an hour that he stared at those pages, with a look on his face that I could not understand. At last he raised his eyes, and said, in a very peculiar tone, "Isabella, you may come here and see if you recognize the words that are in your story." I know that my face was very pale, and I suppose I was as near fainting as I ever reached in my girlhood. I took hold of the molding which ran round the side of the room, to steady me as I walked toward the desk. What do you think I saw lying on the professor's knee? It was a copy of Webster's Dictionary, Unabridged. Of course there was a sense in which what Phebe said was true; every single word of my story was in it.

A GLIMPSE INTO THE FUTURE.

THEY were on their way to a May party. Not such a party as our grandmothers tell about, when they dressed in white and wore wreaths of flowers on their heads, and spent the day in the woods, with a May queen on her throne, and a May-pole to dance about. All those good times, I am afraid, are gone. If we undertook such a celebration as early as the first of May, in most portions of our country, sore throats and coughs would be the result.

Cassie Andrews and Eva Myers were much too sensible young ladies to attempt any such May party. The truth is, they were older at fifteen than their grandmothers at the same age thought of being. They were dressed in their prettiest spring suits, and on their way to a five-o'clock tea at the home of one of their classmates. They had been sauntering along chatting about the girls, and the lovely weather, and the next musicale, and wondering whether Stella Roberts would get a chance to play a duet with the new scholar, who played so magnificently. Suddenly Eva said: "O, Cass, look! there comes crazy Sally. See! she is rigged up like a fortune teller to-day. Oh! isn't she hideous?"

"I'm awfully afraid of her," said Cassie; "I wish we didn't have to meet her in this lonely place. Doesn't she frighten you dreadfully?"

"Not a bit," said Eva, although her eyes looked larger than usual, and she kept her gaze fixed on the ugly-looking old woman who was approaching from the opposite direction; "she is quite harmless, you know; never does anything worse than to get angry and scold like a tornado. I rather like to hear her go on. When she takes a fancy to turn witch she is too queer for anything. And she does tell some very queer things. I never had my fortune told — mamma isn't willing to have me — but when Kate Weston was visiting at our house last winter — you know what a wild girl she is? — well, she was determined to make crazy Sally a visit. Mamma advised her not to, and papa said I couldn't go with her, because it was best to keep away from insane people who lived alone in out-of-the-way places; he said one never knew what strange idea might get possession of them; but Kate was not to be coaxed or advised from carrying out her plans. When my brother Roger came home for Christmas she got him to take her out there one day, and she gave Sally a gold dollar to tell her fortune. Kate has plenty of money, you know, and doesn't understand how to take care of it. Roger said Sally's eyes looked larger than ever; he didn't suppose she had ever before had so much money given her at one time. She ought to have told Kate something pleasant to pay for it; but she didn't. Kate's eyes showed when she came home that she had been crying, and she cried two or three times that night. She never told me the whole of what Sally said; but the part which made her cry was about her mother. Sally said her mother would not live to see the roses in her front yard bloom; and in just two weeks from that day Kate was sent for to go home, and her mother died within two hours after she reached there. Wasn't that strange? How do you suppose crazy Sally knew anything about it?"

"She didn't, of course," said Cassie promptly; "it was what our "Mental Philosophy" calls a coincidence, you know; I am sure it gives several instances more striking than that. But it was sad for poor Kate. I shouldn't like to hear such a thing as that about my mother when I was away from her, even though it came from only a crazy person."

"Well," said Eva, "I can't help wishing mamma would let me try my fortune, just to see what she would say. What harm could it do? and it would be such fun to keep watch and see if any of the things she predicted happened to you. Let us stop and speak to her, Cassie. Sometimes she says the cutest things."

Cassie, half-fearful, yet unwilling to own to fear about a person who was said to be harmless, could do no other than stop, as crazy Sally came directly in front of them, nodded her head several times, and held out her hand toward Cassie, muttering as she did so: "Pretty missy, very pretty missy indeed; got a hand that shows a fortune worth hearing. Give Sally a piece of money large enough to cover her thumb, and she will tell pretty missy something that she will like to know."

Cassie allowed her hand to be held by the strange-looking woman, partly because she was afraid to take it away, and partly because there was a fascination in the wild eyes into which she could not help staring with her own great brown ones. Eva nudged her arm. "O, Cassie! do let her, just for fun. Your mother has never told you not to, has she? I should just like to hear what she would say."

"Pretty missy need not be afraid," said Sally; "she has a very pretty fortune, and it is coming fast. I can tell her all about it."

"Oh!" said Cassie, "I can't; papa would not like it, I know. Let us go on, Eva."

"I'm almost afraid to go on," said Eva, "without giving her something, or letting her do as she wants to; it might make her angry, and sometimes she chases people."

All this was spoken in undertone, while Sally was muttering and mumbling over the hand she held.

"O, dear!" said Cassie, "I am frightened; let us run."

"No," answered Eva decidedly, "we must not do that; she will be sure to chase us, and there isn't a house within some distance, you know. I forgot Sally had put up her tent this spring, or we wouldn't have come this way."

"Good afternoon, young ladies," said a pleasant voice just behind them, and to Cassie's unutterable relief Professor Dickson appeared in sight, and fixed his keen gray eyes on Sally as he spoke; "what is all this?"

"O, Professor Dickson!" said Cassie, "we are so glad to see you. Sally wants to tell my fortune, and I don't want it told."

"Not by her, I trust," said the professor quickly. "Never mind, Sally," he added, gently pushing her hand away from the girl's trembling one; "the young lady does not want to hear what you think of her future, and she has no money for you. Stand aside, and let us pass."

Crazy Sally looked angry; but the professor's voice was firm, and his gray eyes were looking steadily at her. She obeyed, but muttered fierce threats against them all, as she moved sullenly toward her tent, and the three walked briskly away.

"I wouldn't have dared to speak sharply to her," said Eva. "They say she never hurts anybody, but she talks so dreadfully when she is angry."

"I sometimes fear that poor Sally is more wicked than crazy," said Professor Dickson. "Undoubtedly she is not entirely responsible for her acts, but this habit of giving her money to tell them false things about their future is injurious to her as well as to them."

Eva and Cassie exchanged glances, and Cassie wondered if her friend remembered she had urged her to do just that thing. She was sure she would not like to own it to Professor Dickson. All the girls liked the new professor, who was so young looking that at times it seemed almost amusing to call him by his title. Still he was very dignified, with a gentlemanly dignity which fitted him, and he was polite even to young girls like Eva and Cassie. He never forgot to lift his hat to them, and he always addressed them as "Miss Cassie" and "Miss

Eva." Oh! he was so different from the young men who had grown up in the town, and whom they had always known. Most of them were in the habit of nodding a careless "How d'ye do, Eva," or "Cassie," and some of them who had known her longest even said "Cass" occasionally, an abbreviation which Cassie Andrews hated. Certainly Professor Dickson was very different, and both girls desired to have his good opinion.

Eva, mindful perhaps of her advice to Cassie, tried to uphold it.

"But Professor Dickson, she does say some very strange things; I have known several of her predictions to come true."

"I do not doubt it in the least, Miss Eva. If I should make a prediction that you would be in school to-morrow; that you would enter the classroom just as the bell was ringing for ten, and that you would be thoroughly prepared with your lesson, I should not be surprised to have it 'come true' in every particular."

Eva laughed. This was certainly a pleasant way of ridiculing her statement. "Oh! but I mean other things than those," she said; and then abandoning her position as one which she knew was foolish, she said: "Of course I know things only happen to come to pass as she says; I do not believe in her fortune telling, but I cannot help wishing there were some truth in it. I was telling Cassie a few minutes ago what fun I thought it would be if we could have our fortunes told by somebody who really knew about the future. Then we could watch and see if what had been foretold came to pass. I cannot think of anything more interesting and exciting."

Professor Dickson looked down at the eager face of the young girl with a thoughtful smile, and made no answer for several minutes. Then he said:

"Young ladies, would you be surprised if I should tell you that I was a sort of fortune teller myself?"

"You?" exclaimed both girls in a breath; and their incredulity and amazement were so great that his smile broke into a laugh.

"Perhaps that is not the right way to phrase it, but I really do mean that, given a careful following of the conditions imposed, I can predict with a great degree of certainty the future of some persons; for instance, you two friends."

Eva was the first to speak. "O, Professor Dickson! how perfectly splendid! and will you really do it for us?"

"I said there were conditions, Miss Eva."

"Oh! we will meet the conditions; will we not, Cassie? Crazy Sally has 'conditions,' too," she added with a laugh. "She made Helen Porter walk five times around the school-room yard all alone after dark, and frightened her nearly out of her senses."

"I do not think we need be afraid of any conditions which Professor Dickson will propose," said Cassie. To which Eva assented.

"Very well," said Professor Dickson; "if you are quite agreed as to that, I will prepare each of you a paper containing the conditions, or perhaps we would better call them the prescriptions, which, if obeyed, will result to a certainty in a very wonderful thing, a glimpse or hint of which I will give you. I will have the papers ready by to-morrow morning, and will hand them to you in the history class."

This was certainly interesting. When together they could talk of nothing else, although they resolved to keep the matter a profound secret for the present.

The next morning curious eyes were on the two as they received each, with smiles and blushes, an envelope addressed in Professor Dickson's best style. "I have done my best, young ladies," he said, as he turned away, "and I am prepared to assure you that if you meet the conditions the result is certain."

By mutual consent they waited until they had reached the summer-house at the extreme end of the grounds before they looked into their magic papers.

"What do you suppose it is?" asked Cassie.

"I haven't the least idea," laughed Eva; "I feel sort of creepy, don't you? The idea of looking into a paper which will actually tell us what will happen to us in the future! But how absurd that is! What does Professor Dickson know about the future, any more than we do?"

"I shall meet the conditions, if possible," said Cassie, "and test his knowledge."

"Oh! so shall I, if only for the sake of boasting over his failure." But to this Cassie made no reply; her eyes were fixed upon the sheet of note-paper spread out before her, and the glow on her cheeks was deepening, as she read in Professor Dickson's beautiful writing:

A REVELATION OF MISS CASSIE ANDREWS'S FUTURE.

CONDITIONS.

"What doth the Lord require of thee but to do justly, and to love mercy and to walk humbly with thy God." "Come out from among them, and be ye separate."

"Seek ye the Lord while he may be found; call ye upon him while he is near."

THE REVELATION.

"And I will receive you; and I will be to you a father; and ye shall be to me sons and daughters, saith the Lord Almighty."

"The King's daughter within the palace is all glorious; her clothing is inwrought with gold; she shall be led unto the King in 'broidered work. Her companions that follow her shall be brought unto thee; with gladness and rejoicing shall they be led; they shall enter into the King's palace."

Three times did the girls read this; read it at last with eyes which were dimmed with tears. They had no difficulty in understanding it. They had been well taught, and they knew only too well that up to this time they had passed by the many invitations of this wonderful King unheeded. It had never seemed so strange a thing as it did at this moment.

"Eva," said Cassie at last, speaking softly, "we pledged ourselves to meet the conditions."

"I know it," said Eva. "O, Cassie! we will keep our word. It is wonderful, but we do know what our future may be, after all."

"Shall be," said Cassie, with quiet decision.

THE TRAINED NURSE.

IT began when she was only ten; and it grew out of a remark made about her new cap. She remembered the day vividly; it was her birthday, and among her gifts was that one of a soft white silk cap with a lovely pink ribbon twisted carelessly about its front. A fancy cap, of course, to be used in the entertainment called "Costumes and Customs of all Nations," which was being gotten up in Winnie's society. Poor Winnie had been in anxiety for several days lest her mother would think a white silk cap with broad pink ribbon wound about it, much too expensive an article for one entertainment. She did say it was foolish, and that white muslin and pink tarletan would do just as well as silk and ribbon. But there was a foolish auntie in the home who could not help wanting Winnie to have everything that she wanted, so the silk cap with its broad soft pink ribbon was forthcoming on the birthday morning, and Winnie arrayed herself in it and went to the sewing-room to exhibit. She was greeted with bursts of laughter.

"A little Greek maiden," said Auntie Kate.

"An Irish girl," said cousin Tom, who was loitering in the sewing-room snipping bits of thread over his cousin Alice's dress. "See, it brings out the Irish likeness that I have always contended was hovering about in Aunt Winifred's family."

"She looks like a little trained nurse," said her mother. And this was the remark which had arrested Winnie's thoughts.

"A trained nurse?" she repeated. "Trained for what, mother?"

"Why, to take care of sick people, dear; they go to schools established for the purpose, and learn how to care for the sick — how to bathe and feed them, you know, and arrange their pillows and do everything to make them comfortable. They are great blessings to the world."

"And do they wear white silk caps with pink ribbons?"

"Hardly; they are much more sensible. But they wear pretty white caps of muslin or lawn, nicely starched; and they wear white aprons and soft shoes which make no noise, and they know just how warm the room should be kept, and just what window to lower, and just how to shade the light, and do everything to add to one's comfort."

Now Winnie had had from her very babyhood a fondness for playing that she was a famous doctor who could with a word and a touch cure people who were thought to be almost past cure. But she lived in a part of the world and at a time when a lady physician was almost a curiosity; so as she grew older she used often to think with a sigh that it must all be play; that being a girl instead of a boy she could not go to college and study medicine and become the great doctor of her dreams. Some women did; she had heard of but never seen one, and her mother she felt sure would not like it. She must just give up playing that, and put away her powders and phials. On this birthday morning the mother's words about trained nurses were a revelation. There was a chance then to distinguish herself in the very line which she coveted. To be such a trained nurse as her mother had described, to know all those things, and to be called "a great blessing" by such a woman as her mother, Winnie judged was distinction enough for any woman. She paid little heed to the merry talk which went on about her cap, her mind being full of the new thought; and before the morning was over she had determined what she would do in the world—she would be a trained nurse.

In the course of the next few days Winnie contrived to get much further information from her mother in regard to the matter. Particularly she was interested in the kind of caps the nurses wore, and being skillful with both scissors and needle, in the course of the next week she had fashioned some very creditable caps of white lawn and adorned her choicest dolls with them. From that time on Winifred had a new ambition. The family were greatly amused with it for a time, and called her "Nurse," but after awhile they forgot all about it; not so Winnie. As she grew older her interest in nurses and nursing increased rather than diminished. She cut from the daily papers every scrap which she saw on the subject; she listened attentively to the talk of Dr. Benson when he called, in the hope that something professional would creep in; she brought from the library popular works on health and disease, and not only read but studied them to such purpose that after awhile she really became an authority in the matter of slight bruises, burns, and the like. "Ask Winnie what to do for it," became a common sentence in the household. Long after the white silk cap had been made into dress trimmings, and the pink ribbon had done duty as a willow basket ornament, the lesson which had been connected with them staid by Winnie and grew with her growth. It was almost a trial to her that theirs was such a healthful household, that there was really no opportunity for practicing her arts. It was not that she wished people to be sick, but if they had to be at any time, she could not help wishing it would come while she was so ready and willing to serve. But the years passed, and beyond a few toothaches and a headache now and then, no one in the family connection had suffered, save Winnie herself; she, in the meantime, had measles and scarlet fever; and being waited upon for two days while her mother was resting, by Betsey Hawkins from the kitchen, Winnie confided to her mother that she had learned how not to do a good many things.

It was when Winnie had passed her fourteenth year and was grown a tall capable girl, and had packed away all her dolls because there was really no time to play with them, that her opportunity came.

Came in a most romantic manner, which made it of still more interest; for Winnie, I am obliged to confess, had a touch of the romantic about her.

A man on horseback was galloping by, and came in contact with the steam fire-engine just at the corner; the horse was frightened and reared and plunged and finally threw the man, who was past middle age and not much used to horseback riding. He fell heavily, hitting his head against the curbstone as he did so; Winifred's father was the first man at his side, being just on his way home, and it naturally followed that the wounded man was carried to his own house. It was Winnie who ran upstairs to open the spare chamber, and draw down the shades, and make the bed ready for its occupant. It was she who hovered about Dr. Benson for the first few minutes after he arrived, getting him water, and the scissors, and several other things for which he called. Her mother was out when the accident occurred, and Winnie was in the hall explaining matters to her when Dr. Benson came out of the spare room.

"We shall have to make a private hospital of your house for a time, I fear," he said; "the man is a stranger in town, I fancy. He is not able to speak, but I know most persons in or about this region, and I have never seen him before. He is quite badly hurt; not fatally, I think; but he must not be moved for weeks; and will probably need a great deal of care."

Of course both Mr. and Mrs. Holden declared themselves ready to do everything in their power; and the doctor went away to try to find a professional nurse. Early the next morning he encountered Winnie on the stairs arrayed in a new fashion. A large white apron very clean and neat covered her dress in front entirely, the bib being fastened high enough to show only the frill of her gingham dress; and on her head was a dainty little lawn cap for all the world like the professional ones.

The doctor stopped and surveyed her from head to foot.

"A trained nurse, I declare!" he said, with a surprised little laugh; "I am extremely glad to see you, for my patient is delirious this morning, and has taken a dislike to the one I have provided. Perhaps you can coax him to fancy you. Even an insane man might do that, I should think."

Winnie knew he was laughing at her, but she kept her grave face.

"I thought I might be of use," she said with dignity, "and I might as well put on my cap and gown; I have had them ready a long time, and I know how to do a good many things for sick people."

The doctor's words, spoken in jest, proved to

be more true than he had imagined. The sick man, whose brain was full of all sorts of queer conceits, took an instant fancy to the young, fresh face looking gravely out at him from under its quaint little cap. He accepted with a gracious smile the soothing draught which the doctor handed her to give him, notwithstanding the fact that he had imperiously refused to take it at the hands of either doctor or professional nurse. For the next two weeks Winnie certainly had a taste of genuine nursing. The delirious patient would have his medicine and his nourishment at her hands and none other. He would permit her to bathe his head and cool his pillow, and do anything for him indeed that she chose to do.

"A born nurse!" said Dr. Benson to her mother, who was half-annoyed and half-amused at the composed way in which Winnie had superseded the doctor's professional nurse, so that she had little to do in the daytime.

"You ought to let her take a thorough course of training. She would be invaluable in the sick room; she has just the gentle and yet quick touch which a patient appreciates. Very slow movements often irritate a nervous person, and not one nurse in twenty knows how to be quick, and quiet, and gentle at the same time. That little woman in cap and white gown is a treasure."

So the invalid thought, as the weeks passed. There came a day when he was quite himself, but all the morning he appeared to be watching for somebody, and at last he asked where the little white-capped maid was, and Winnie was summoned. From that hour they became warm friends; nobody could comb the threads of gray hair on the man's head, or arrange the pillows for it, or do any of those numberless small things which sick people want, equal to Winnie.

Meantime, Winnie's thoughts had been very busy during this time of responsibility. She had other ambitions than merely to nurse bodies. Was her dear gray-haired patient a Christian? This was the question which daily haunted her. There had been a time when she was in terror lest he might die, and she never know; now she feared he might get well and go away without her having discovered whether he belonged to Christ. That, to Winnie's mind,

THE LITTLE WHITE-CAPPED MAID.

was very defective nursing; yet the doctor had given strict orders that his patient must not be excited in any way. At last the day came when the sick man wanted to be read to, and Winnie was chosen as reader. After reading for an hour in the daily papers, turning to whatever page or column was demanded, Winnie asked: "May I read to you a little bit out of the Bible now, sir?"

He turned a pair of great gray eyes upon her and asked briefly, "Why?"

"Why, because you have been sick a long time and must have missed it if you are used to it, and if not"—she stopped, but he was still looking at her her.

"Well," he said after a minute, "and if not, what then?"

"Why, then you have missed it without knowing it, and that is worse."

He laughed a little over this; said it was "sharp," and after a moment asked if it would give her any pleasure to read to him out of the Bible; if it would, he was willing to listen simply to please her, for she had been a very good friend to him; indeed, he did not know what he would have done without her; but it had been years since he had listened to the Bible, except occasionally in church.

So the Bible readings were commenced, and went on every evening; Winnie being sometimes stopped abruptly and asked what she thought such a verse meant, and if she knew any people who acted as the Bible said they must. It was this question in some form or other which seemed most to trouble her patient. At last one evening she said: "I know people who try to do as the Bible wants them to, but if I didn't know a single person it would make no difference, so long as I knew Jesus. If there was nobody trying to get rich, and yet I knew there was money to be had, I think I should try for it all the same." After that he told her again that she was "pretty sharp," and then he lay quite still and seemed to be listening to the Bible words.

"I will tell you something," he said to Winnie one morning; he was looking better than he had before, and Winnie knew that the doctor called him almost well; "something that I think will please you: a little maid like you used to love to read and study her Bible; she was my little girl. I would not let her read the Bible to me, but I made no objection to her reading it herself; she loved it and tried to live by it. She was all I had; one day she died. I was angry about it, and said God was cruel to take all I had, and that I would never serve him. I lived without him for years, though I knew it would hurt my little girl if she were here. I got on as best I could until he had pity on me and let me be thrown from a horse in front of a home where was another little woman like my daughter; she has coaxed me back to life and coaxed me back to God. I have known how to serve him ever since I was a child; now I am going to do it; and it is my little trained nurse who has led me."

"Mother," said Winnie, "I do truly think God put the desire to take care of sick people into my heart, so I could work for him in this way. And to think he has given me my first patient. Don't you believe he did it to encourage me in my life-work?"

Yes, it is her life-work. She is a trained nurse now, and people when they have very sick friends say: "Oh! if we can only get Miss Winifred Holden to take care of her."

I am not sure that Mrs. Holden is even yet quite reconciled to it; she very much wanted Winnie to be a lady of leisure, and live in a grand house, and do good with her money. "But I brought it on myself," she said once, half-laughing. "Winnie says it was a foolish little remark which I made about a fancy cap she had, which set her heart in that way. It only shows how careful we ought to be of our words. They accomplish, sometimes, things which we had no idea of."

AN ADAPTED COLLOQUY.

IT did not surprise any one that Edward Parker and Annie Webster were chosen to represent their grade in the coming prize contest. They had agreed between themselves to choose a colloquy for their recitation. "Something which had real sound temperance argument in it," Edward stipulated, "that would do people good to listen to, even though they didn't enjoy the way it was said. But then, Annie, if it should happen that we should take the prize, how would we manage?"

"Why, divide it," replied Annie. "The money prize is a ten-dollar gold piece, and that will make two fives; but I haven't the least idea that we will take the prize. Harvey Morrison is going to try for it, you know, and you say yourself that he is the best speaker among the boys. And Doris Hanley is going to try, so where is the chance for us?"

"All right," said Edward, "all the more reason why we should select first class material, that will be well worth listening to."

They spent days in hunting for a colloquy on temperance which satisfied them; but at last they chose a discussion between two young people about the wisdom, or the folly, of signing the pledge; and having prepared their parts with great care, they met on this first afternoon to rehearse. They were old friends, these two, were nearly of an age, and had been playmates even in their babyhood. They were perfectly frank in conversation, and good-naturedly told each other some plain truths. For instance, over one response which "Kent," a boy in the colloquy, had made, Annie laughed merrily. "If 'Kent' talked like that, Edward, I am not surprised that the girl called him a 'noodle.'" ("Emma" was the girl in the colloquy.) "It may not have been very polite, but it was expressive. You don't say it the least bit like yourself, Edward; I shouldn't know it was you talking. You don't even speak in a natural tone of voice. I'll tell you just how you said it."

And she mimicked the rapid, slightly singsong, parrot-like style which Edward had used. He joined in her laugh, although his cheeks grew red.

"That's being pretty hard on a fellow, Annie. I don't believe that girl in the colloquy ever talked so to Kent. I know I wasn't natural; I cannot be. I will tell you what the trouble is; it is not a natural sentence. Who ever heard a fellow of my age getting off a sentence like that, full of big words?" and he mimicked the supposed speaker. "'The truth is, my dear friend, we are compelled by existing circumstances to make constant practical application of the pledge idea, in the complications of an ordinary business life.' I don't believe he ever said any such thing! It doesn't sound like a fellow who knew what he was talking about. Imagine me getting off such a sentence as that to you! If he knew enough, he would say that every time a fellow offered a banknote he had either accepted a pledge, or else he was a scamp. 'Compelled by existing circumstances!' Existing fiddlesticks! Why can't they put common sense into colloquys, I wonder, and say things as boys and girls say them, instead of making a boy of thirteen talk like his grandfather?"

"And the girl is just as bad," said Annie; "she talks like her great-aunt oftener than she does like herself. I'll tell you what it is, Edward, I have an idea. Let us go over this thing and strike out all the sentences which sound unnatural — unlike a girl and boy — and put in the words we believe we would have said if we had been arguing about the pledge. To be sure, you and I are both on the same side, but then we can imagine how we would talk if we weren't. I shouldn't wonder if we had as much sense as this 'Kent' and 'Emma,' whoever they were; and I'm sure we know how to use smaller words than they. Then perhaps we can both be natural. You did not criticise me, Edward; but you ought to have done so. I felt all the time that I was not being natural; I could not help speaking some of those sentences in a sort of affected grown-up tone, just because they are 'grown-up' sentences, instead of being such as a girl would use. I never thought what the trouble was until you suggested it. I propose that we make this colloquy over."

"All right," said Edward; "let's go in. I always thought I should like to write something to be printed. This is print, and if we make it over we have the right to call ourselves the authors, haven't we?"

"We can do as they do with hymns that they mend," said Annie, laughing, "A colloquy on the pledge, 'adapted' by Edward Parker and Annie Webster."

There was a good deal more talk and laughter, but better than these, there was good work done. The two were fair thinkers, and good writers for their ages; moreover, they knew how girls and boys talked when they were together. They went over the colloquy sentence by sentence, striking out all the long words, re-arranging the involved sentences, making them sound simple and natural. Some of the sentences they omitted altogether, as unreasonable, considering the supposed age of the speakers.

"Now," said Annie, when an hour's work had been done, "I believe this is going to be a success. I feel less stiff already; it seems so much more natural to say, 'O, Kent! I wish you wouldn't talk such nonsense,' than to say, as that dreadful little prig of an 'Emma' did, 'I am very sorry indeed to hear you converse upon these themes in such an unreasonable manner.' Think of me getting that off, Edward," and she laughed merrily.

"Well," said Edward, "it is so entirely changed that it amounts to a new colloquy. We will each have to go home and set to work to learn it."

"It will be easily learned," said Annie, looking it over with much satisfaction. "Some of the sentences we shall remember, because we made them word for word, and the others sound so like us that we cannot help thinking of them. I think it is a real splendid way of making a colloquy. Take one that is all prinked up stiff and prim, and as unlike yourself as possible, but which has good thoughts which can be put into the words you would use if you were going to say them. Perhaps we have invented something new under the sun, Edward, and shall get famous."

"If we get the prize I shall be satisfied," said Edward, as he took his copy of the very much interlined colloquy, and marched away. They were gay and meaningless words; neither he nor Annie had, as they had said, the least idea of securing the prize. Were there not much older and wiser people than they on the list of contestants? Nevertheless they were deeply interested in what they called their reconstructed colloquy; and now that it sounded natural, they talked it off to each other exactly as though they were having a chat together.

"I never heard anything more naturally done," said one of the teachers to them on the evening of the contest, as Edward and Annie, having given their colloquy, returned to their seats near her side. "Part of the time I actually forgot that you were reciting a colloquy; it seemed just as though you were chatting together, and I happened to hear it. I don't understand how you managed to be so natural."

"Because we said natural things," answered Annie, smiling and pleased; this was a favorite teacher, and her commendation was worth much more. "It is just as Edward and I talk together, only he doesn't use such absurd arguments as that 'Kent' did; but he would put them into those words if he did. I hope Professor Durand liked it. He said he was afraid the younger ones who had no expectation of getting the prize would not make much effort, but Edward and I did our best. Didn't Doris Hanley recite beautifully? Don't you believe she will get it?"

This conversation was held while the band was playing, and the audience was waiting for the prize to be awarded. Presently all was quiet, for the chairman of the committee of award was on his feet. I think the only astonished people in the room were Edward and Annie, when their names were called.

"We actually got it," said Annie.

"We did that!" said Edward. "Let's 'adapt' something else sometime."

HOW BARBARA HELPED.

MISS FANNIE FLETCHER'S dress looked very cool and summery as she ran down the steps to meet the boat which Peter Dunlap was skillfully steering toward her, but there was not a pleasant look on her face. There were lines across her forehead and about her mouth which told of a ruffled spirit. The truth is, Miss Fannie had had anything but a pleasant time that morning. The entire family were in the country for the summer, and the family was large. There were three or four little Fletchers, and two grown-up sons, with only one grown-up daughter, so there was, of course, a great deal of work to be done in the country home, and not very good help to depend upon. Mrs. Fletcher had come into Fannie's room just after breakfast, looking greatly worried.

"I don't know how to plan," she said. "Jane has the ironing to finish which she left yesterday, you know, when company came; and Katie has hurt her foot, and cannot run after Baby at all, and I must be upstairs with Lucy most of the time, for she is not so well to-day. Now, in addition to all the rest, comes a note from Harry, saying he has met two of his college friends, and will bring them out to dinner."

"Dear me!" said Fannie, hurrying into her freshly-ironed white dress, "that is just like Harry, always piling company on us whether it is convenient or not. Why couldn't he have let them get their dinner at the Lake House, and make their call here afterward?"

"I suppose he did not like to do that, since they are strangers here," returned the mother, and added hesitatingly: "Couldn't you plan in some way to help Jane with the dinner? If you could look after the dessert, and help a little about the vegetables, she could manage the rest."

"Why, mother, how could I?" asked Fannie, stopping in the act of arranging her collar to ask the question. "I am very late now; I presume Peter has been waiting for me for some time, and we are not to come home until just dinner time. I don't see how I can be depended upon. If Katie hadn't been a simpleton she would not have hurt her foot. It seems to me we have the most accidents of any family I ever heard of."

"Katie did not mean to be careless, dear; I thought perhaps you could delay starting for an hour or two, and help get things under way. Or you might give up the idea of a picnic for this time. It will be very warm in the glen to-day. I should think it would be much pleasanter to go when there was more air stirring. If you would just go for a little ride on the lake, and stop at the glen for a few minutes, then you could take Baby along; he would enjoy it wonderfully, and you could get back in ample time for helping with the dinner."

But the frowns on her daughter's face only deepened.

"The idea!" she said. "How very strange it is that you think I can overturn all my plans for the sake of helping Jane get dinner. It seems to me you forget that it is my Sunday-school class, and that they have been invited by me to spend the day at the glen. I have to keep my word, don't I? especially with girls whom I am trying to help. I don't know another young lady from town who has taken a summer class in Sunday-school. When I am trying to do all I can, I should think I might have some encouragement."

"I know, dear," Mrs. Fletcher said soothingly; "you are very active. But the circumstances are peculiar, you know; if Lucy were well enough to be left alone I might manage, or if it were not for Baby, perhaps I could. I thought since there were only four girls, and two of them from the same family, another day might do as well for them, especially if you explained to them how it was."

Miss Fannie was ready now, even to her gloves and sun umbrella.

"I cannot think of such a thing," she said decidedly. "I am sorry about it all, I am sure; and I don't think Harry need have been so selfish; and Jane might have gotten the ironing out of the way if she had tried very hard. But there is no use in talking about my putting off the picnic. It is chiefly gotten up for Barbara Dunlap; and she, you know, has just come into the Sunday-school, and started to be a Christian. What would she think of me?

"No, Baby, I cannot take you with me, and there is no use in crying about it. Take him back to the house, Katie; you ought not to have let him follow me. I cannot help it if your foot does hurt; you need not have been so careless."

This last sentence was spoken after she reached the landing, just as Peter Dunlap was bringing his boat around. The frowns on Miss Fannie's face had deepened. It certainly was not pleasant to have Baby screaming after her. He was two years and three months old, and had excellent lungs, and was fond of boating.

"Such a fuss to get started," she said, with a sigh of disgust. "It is enough to make one shrink from trying to do anything. Be still, Prince! of course you can go when the boat gets here, but there is no use in barking about it."

"Uncle Joseph" was looking gloomily out of the window at her. He was not her uncle, but everybody by force of habit called him "uncle." He was the sick and miserable brother of the woman who kept the Lake House. Fannie had been talking with him but the day before, trying to convince him that he ought to be a Christian.

"There's your Christianity," he told himself sneeringly. "She can take Prince and go off for a day's pleasuring, and leave her baby brother screaming after her, with no one but that little lame girl to look after him, and the mother with more work to do than she can manage, I'll warrant. I heard her wondering how it was all going to get done."

Just at that moment Miss Fannie discovered that Peter Dunlap was alone. "Why, where are Barbara and Bess?" she asked, stopping half-way down the steps. "I do hope we have not to be delayed by your going back after them; it is very late now."

"No, ma'am," said Peter; "they won't hinder you. Barbara sent word that she was very sorry, but she could not go to-day; and of course little Bess could not go without her."

"Not go?" said Miss Fannie; "why, what

does the child mean? I was going for her sake chiefly."

"Well, ma'am," said Peter, "I am very sorry, and I think Barbara felt it more than she would own; but you see, ma'am, my wife is bad off to-day with one of her headaches, and Barbara she said she couldn't go and leave her with the baby to look after. She is along in years, you know, ma'am, and three children to take care of is a good deal, though Barbara is a little woman, and has been ever since her mother died; but the baby is mischievous, and when his grandmother has the headache he is hard on her. She urged Barbara to go, and said she could get along. But Barbara wouldn't hear a word to it. 'Grandmother,' says she, 'Miss Fletcher would be ashamed of me if I ran away to a picnic and shirked my duty.' But to me she said, 'Grandfather, I couldn't go, you know, because if I am a servant of Jesus Christ I must try to please him in everything, and he wouldn't be pleased to have me leave Bobby with grandmother all day when her head aches, would he?' and I couldn't make no answer to that, so Barbara had her way."

Miss Fannie had no answer to make, either, for several minutes. She stood on the step, her forehead still wrinkled, but her face growing quieter and sweeter. At last she said, "Very well, Peter, wait for me a few minutes." Then running up the steps she looked down the road leading to the house. In the distance was Dick, the errand boy at the Lake House. She motioned him to her. "Dick, just run to our house and bring Baby to me, will you? Tell mamma I am going to take him for a little ride in the boat, and I will come back in time to see to everything about dinner. And be as quick as you can, that's a good boy."

"If I had any religion I should want it to be Barbara's kind."

That was what Uncle Joseph muttered to himself when he heard Peter Dunlap's story. But as he watched the boat slip away at last, with the happy "Baby" seated by his sister's side, he was forced to add: "Perhaps Miss Fannie's kind isn't bad to have, when she stops to think about what she is doing."

The Pansy Books

By MRS. G. R. ALDEN ("PANSY")

PANSY
Trade-mark registered June 4, 1895

$1.50 per volume

1. As in a Mirror
2. Aunt Hannah, Martha and John
3. By Way of the Wilderness
4. Chautauqua Girls at Home
5. Chrissy's Endeavor
6. Christie's Christmas
7. Eighty-Seven
8. Endless Chain (An)
9. Ester Ried
10. Ester Ried Yet Speaking
11. Four Girls at Chautauqua
12. Hall in the Grove (The)
13. Her Associate Members
14. Household Puzzles
15. Interrupted
16. John Remington, Martyr
17. Judge Burnham's Daughters
18. Julia Ried
19. King's Daughters
20. Links in Rebecca's Life
21. Little Fishers and Their Nets
22. Mag and Margaret
23. Making Fate
24. Man of the House
25. Mrs. Solomon Smith Looking On
26. New Graft on the Family Tree (A)
27. One Commonplace Day
28. Overruled
29. Pauline
30. Pocket Measure (The)
31. Prince of Peace
32. Randolphs (The)
33. Ruth Erskine's Crosses
34. Sevenfold Trouble (A)
35. Spun from Fact
36. Stephen Mitchell's Journey
37. Those Boys
38. Three People
39. Tip Lewis and His Lamp
40. Twenty Minutes Late
41. Unto the End
42. Wanted
43. What They Couldn't
44. Wise and Otherwise
45. Yesterdays Framed in Today

$1.25 per volume

46. Cunning Workmen
47. Divers Women
48. Echoing and Reëchoing.
49. From Different Standpoints
50. Grandpa's Darlings
51. Miss Dee Dunmore Bryant
52. Modern Exodus (A)
53. Modern Prophets
54. Only Ten Cents
55. Profiles
56. Reuben's Hindrances
57. Sidney Martin's Christmas

Lothrop Publishing Company - - Boston

The Pansy Books

By MRS. G. R. ALDEN ("PANSY")

PANSY
Trade-mark registered June 4, 1895

$1.00 per volume

58. Dr. Deane's Way
59. Miss Priscilla Hunter
60. Mrs. Deane's Way
61. What She Said

75 cents per volume

62. At Home and Abroad
63. Bobby's Wolf
64. Couldn't Be Bought
65. Five Friends
66. In the Woods and Out
67. Jessie Wells
68. Missent
69. Modern Sacrifice
70. Mrs. Harry Harper
71. New Year's Tangles
72. Next Things
73. Older Brother (The)
74. Pansy's Scrap Book
75. Some Young Heroines
76. Worth Having
77. Young Folks Worth Knowing

60 cents per volume

78. Bernie's White Chicken
79. Docia's Journal
80. Getting Ahead
81. Helen Lester
82. Mary Burton Abroad
83. Monteagle
84. Pansies
85. Six Little Girls
86. Stories Told for a Purpose
87. That Boy Bob
88. Two Boys

50 cents per volume

89. Browning Boys (The)
90. Dozen of Them (A)
91. Exact Truth (The)
92. Gertrude's Diary
93. Glimpses of Boyhood
94. Glimpses of Girlhood
95. Grace Holbrook
96. Hedge Fence
97. Helen the Historian
98. Her Mother's Bible
99. Kaleidoscope (The)
100. Little Card (The)
101. Side by Side
102. Six O'Clock in the Evening
103. Stories from the Life of Jesus
104. Stories of Great Men
105. Stories of Remarkable Women
106. Story of Puff
107. Their Vacation
108. We Twelve Girls
109. World of Little People (A)

Lothrop Publishing Company - - Boston

The Famous Pepper Books

By MARGARET SIDNEY

FIVE LITTLE PEPPERS AND HOW THEY GREW
12mo, cloth, illustrated, $1.50.

"A genuine child classic."

FIVE LITTLE PEPPERS MIDWAY
12mo, cloth, illustrated, $1.50.

"Every page is full of sunshine." — *Detroit Press.*

FIVE LITTLE PEPPERS GROWN UP
12mo, cloth, illustrated, $1.50.

"The tale sparkles with life and animation. The young people are bright and jolly, and enjoy their lives as everybody ought to do." — *Woman's Journal.*

PHRONSIE PEPPER
12mo, cloth. Illustrated by Jessie McDermott. $1.50

This book is the story of Phronsie, the youngest and dearest of all the Peppers.

THE STORIES POLLY PEPPER TOLD
12mo, cloth. Illustrated by Jessie McDermott and Etheldred B Barry. $1.50.

Wherever there exists a child or a "grown-up" to whom the Pepper family has become dear, there is a loving and vociferous welcome for these charming, characteristic, and delightful "Stories Polly Pepper Told."

THE ADVENTURES OF JOEL PEPPER
12mo, cloth. Illustrated by Sears Gallagher. $1.50.

This Pepper book is just as bright and just as much a child's favorite as the others in the famous series. Harum-scarum "Joey" is a lovable boy.

FIVE LITTLE PEPPERS ABROAD
12mo, cloth. Illustrated by Fanny Cory. $1.10 net. Postpaid, $1.25.

In new scenes and new experiences the brightness, the wit, the kindliness, the keen knowledge of child nature that have made all the Pepper Books so irresistible, are just as conspicuous as they have been in the Pepper stories at home.

Lothrop Publishing Company - - Boston

George Cary Eggleston's Juveniles

The Bale Marked Circle X
A Blockade Running Adventure

Illustrated by C. Chase Emerson. 12mo, red cloth, illustrated cover. Net, $1.20. Postpaid, $1.35.

Another of Mr. Eggleston's stirring books for youth. In it are told the adventures of three boy soldiers in the Confederate Service who are sent in a sloop on a secret voyage from Charleston to the Bahamas, conveying a strange bale of cotton which holds important documents. The boys pass through startling adventures: they run the blockade, suffer shipwreck, and finally reach their destination after the pluckiest kind of effort.

Camp Venture
A Story of the Virginia Mountains

Illustrated by W. A. McCullough. 12mo, dark red cloth, illustrated cover, $1.50.

The *Louisville Courier Journal* says: "George Cary Eggleston has written a decidedly good tale of pluck and adventure in 'Camp Venture.' It will be of interest to young and old who enjoy an exciting story, but there is also a great deal of instruction and information in the book."

The Last of the Flatboats
A Story of the Mississippi

Illustrated by Charlotte Harding. 12mo, green cloth, illustrated cover, $1.50.

The *Brooklyn Eagle* says: "Mr. George Cary Eggleston, the veteran editor and author, has scored a double success in his new book, 'The Last of the Flatboats,' which has just been published. Written primarily as a story for young readers, it contains many things that are of interest to older people. Altogether, it is a mighty good story, and well worth reading."

Lothrop Publishing Company - - Boston

www.ingramcontent.com/pod-product-compliance
Lightning Source LLC
Chambersburg PA
CBHW021919180426
43199CB00032B/930